FAMILY
PRACTICE

FAMILY PRACTICE

God's Prescription
for a Healthy Home

EDITED BY
R.C. SPROUL, JR.

P&R
PUBLISHING
P.O. BOX 817 • PHILLIPSBURG • NEW JERSEY 08865-0817

Page design by Tobias Design
Typesetting by Michelle Feaster

Printed in the United States of America

Chapters 1–3 and 5–12 and appendixes 1–3 first appeared in the January 1996, February 1996, and March 1996 issues of *Tabletalk*, a magazine published by Ligonier Ministries.

Biblical quotations are from *The Holy Bible: The New King James Version* (NKJV) copyright 1979, 1980, 1982 by Thomas Nelson. Used by permission. All rights reserved.

For information about Ligonier Ministries, visit its website:
www.ligonier.org

Library of Congress Cataloging-in-Publication Data

    Family practice: God's prescription for a healthy home / edited by R. C. Sproul, Jr.
       p. cm.
    ISBN 0-87552-498-2 (pbk.)
    1. Family—Religious aspects—Christianity. I. Sproul, R. C. (Robert Craig), 1965-

BT707.7.F36 2001
248.4—dc21

                00-065282

CONTENTS

CONTRIBUTORS

Michael S. Beates and his wife, Mary, are the parents of seven children (four home-grown, three hand-picked). He is dean of students at Reformed Theological Seminary in Orlando.

Elisabeth Elliot is an author, a speaker, and a Woman of Titus Two (WOTT) to thousands of women around the globe.

Gary Ezzo, father and grandfather, is the founder of Growing Families International in Chatsworth, California.

Edna Gerstner was the author of *Idelette* and *Jonathan and Sarah*.

James B. Jordan is the research director of Biblical Horizons Ministries in Niceville, Florida.

Don Kistler is president of Soli Deo Gloria ministries in Pittsburgh, Pennsylvania.

Judy Rogers is a composer and recording artist. Two recent recordings are *If You Love Me* and *Guard Your Heart*. She is also a wife and mother.

Franklin Sanders edits and publishes *The Moneychanger*, a monthly newsletter. He has written and coauthored four books, and lives near Westpoint, Tennessee, with his wife and seven children.

R. C. Sproul is president of Ligonier Ministries, the teacher on Ligonier's daily radio broadcast, *Renewing Your Mind*, and author of more than fifty books.

R. C. Sproul, Jr., is the father of five children, editor of *Tabletalk* magazine, and director of the Highlands Study Center near Meadowview, Virginia.

J. Steven Wilkins is pastor of Auburn Avenue Presbyterian Church in Monroe, Louisiana.

Douglas Wilson is a pastor, author, and educator in Moscow, Idaho.

Nancy Wilson is the mother of three and a regular contributor to *Credenda/Agenda* magazine.

———— ∞∞∞ ————

THE COVENANT
FAMILY

———— ∞∞∞ ————

R. C. SPROUL, JR.

Who are you? The wise know that perhaps the safest answer to that rather blunt inquiry might be, "It depends on whom you ask." My father told me recently of a conversation he once had with a stranger. The man asked, "Are you R. C. Sproul?"

My father replied, "I am an R. C. Sproul."

The man asked, "Are you the R. C. Sproul who writes books?"

My father replied, "I am an R. C. Sproul that writes books."

The man asked, "Are you the R. C. Sproul that is on the radio?"

My father replied, "I am an R. C. Sproul that is on the radio."

The man persisted, "Are you the R. C. Sproul that pastors a church?"

And again, "I am an R. C. Sproul that pastors a church."

I have had essentially the same conversation with many people, but in the end, they're looking for my father. My father and I have a great deal in common. We do much the same kind of work (in the same way that a spaceship is the same kind of thing as a paper airplane). We think alike. We even have the same bubble in the middle of all our shirts—though I can't help it; they're hand-me-downs. We both have lovely and loving wives. I have several sweet children, but he has only one—my sister. My identity is wrapped up in his identity in many ways. But there are differences.

When I speak at a conference, my greatest fear is that many people might be expecting to hear the more eloquent and wise R. C. Sproul. I fear the same with every book that sells with my name on it. We may believe most of the same things, but that doesn't mean I've been given all the gifts he's been given. If you read me or hear me speak, you can expect to get an approximation of what the other R. C. thinks. The difference is in the depth of the wisdom and the skill of the delivery.

There are other differences between us as well. I'm quite sure that the good folks at Mastercard can tell the difference between us, and that they give him considerably more leeway in terms of his credit than they give me. Not only that, but we fit into a very different demographic. My father remembers World War II. I barely remember the POWs coming home from Vietnam. He lived for eight years under the reign of Eisenhower, I under the reign of Reagan. There are differences.

When my father was a boy, he lived with his father, grandmother, and uncle near Pittsburgh. The rest of the relatives were scattered around different suburbs of Pittsburgh. My home, on the other hand, is over seven hundred miles away from my parents and from my wife's parents. My cousins, my wife's cousins, and my children's cousins are all at least several hours away by car.

Those differences are at the same time subtle and terribly important. That Christians have manned the barricades in defense of the nuclear family, in an age where family means whatever you want it to mean, demonstrates that we joined the battle too late. If we in the church can keep husband and wife together, and give them a child or two, we think we're doing well. Only a few generations ago, such was not a family at all, but a poor and lonely band of an almost family. We looked at families in terms of several branches, several generations, all tied into the same root, the patriarch and the matriarch. Now we are rootless. Family means not those with whom we have a God-ordained, inseparable bond, but those with whom we share the same roof for a time.

Even when intact, our nuclear families are torn apart. The work world separates families, as fathers and now mothers brave the traffic to get to their place of labor. Children are shuttled off to daycare or school. The masters of culture separate us as well. When we do gather under one roof, Mommy is reading her *Redbook*, Daddy his *Sports Illustrated*. Princess has her nose buried in *Seventeen*, while Junior reads *Boy's Life*. On the weekends we still go our separate ways. Golf and the women's club, ballet and Little League, and soon our "quality time" is reduced to reading Post-it notes on the fridge giving instructions on reheating supper.

The world is not alone in its guilt on this issue. Sunday morning is not only the most racially segregated day of the week, it is also the most age-segregated. We don't go to church together. We just worship under the same roof. Dad is at his Promise Keepers group, Mom at the Women in the Church meeting, Princess in the youth group, and Junior in children's church. We have been, in the world and in the church, tearing asunder what God has brought together.

Our conception of the family is grounded more in modern American individualism than in the Word of God. We tend to see ourselves by ourselves. Our identity is personal more than familial. Families are a hindrance to the pursuit of freedom. They involve sacrifices and compromises. (Andrew Lytle argued that the American family was destroyed not by Hollywood or Washington, but by central heating. Before its advent, families stayed together by the fire. You could either have peace and warmth, or bicker and be cold.) On our own we can be what we want to be. And so our families are nothing other than shells. Or worse, we substitute for the biblical family our peer group. We identify most with those who fit in our demographic. Each of these identity groups tends to have its own uniforms, music, language, symbols, habits, and bumper stickers.

When the doctor looks in the ears of my children and asks, "Is Barney in there?" he is making an identification. If you don't know who Barney is, it's probably because you're not five. He's a purple, nearly ubiquitous dinosaur that children watch on television or videotapes. The doctor assumes that because my child is six years old, he is enamored with Barney. But my children are Sprouls first, children second. And though they know who Barney is, they know this:

"Sprouls don't much care for Barney the dinosaur. We do care for Deputy Barney Fife." We have lots of videotapes, but they're of the *Andy Griffith Show*, not Barney.

My children are trained to see themselves not as members of a peer group, but as members of our family. We even have a family catechism to match. Ask any of my children his or her name, and they'll tell you, beginning with his or her first name. Next you get the middle name, then "Sproul." Ask them what a Sproul is, and they answer, "Sprouls are free." Ask them who Sprouls serve, and they will tell you, "Sprouls serve Jesus Christ." Ask them what Sprouls fear, and they will tell you, "Sprouls fear no man; Sprouls fear God."

These are not conclusions to which my children have come on their own. Nor are they the result of careful empirical research. My children believe them because they are what Daddy has told them. I confess: I am indoctrinating my children. They're too little to fight back with me, which is just as it should be.

I teach my children these things, and a whole host of other things, about how and why we serve Jesus Christ, about how and why we fear no man. We fear God because we're commanded to do so. I'm in covenant with God, through the work of his Son, and one stipulation of this covenant is that I instruct my children in this covenant.

Covenant is a big theological word. It is a word found frequently in the pages of God's Word. It is a concept that is central to my own theological convictions and to the convictions of a whole school of thought. I remember that frightening day when I was first examined to see if I was ready to become a pastor. In most if not all Presbyterian denominations, the process involves an oral exam, given in the presence of a roomful of godly men. They asked me all manner of questions, seeking to find out two important things. First, do I affirm any serious theological errors? They can't approve me to be a pastor if, for instance, I affirm that a person is made right with God through refusing to eat meat. And second, do I know what I ought to know? They asked me to outline the Gospel of John. They asked me about the great chain of salvation in Romans 8. And they asked me to list the covenants God made with man. I listed them off: "There is the covenant with Adam. There is the covenant with Noah. There is the Abrahamic covenant. There is the covenant with David. . . ."

My wife, sitting in a pew, overheard one man say to another, "He forgot the covenant with Abraham." I'm not sure if the gentleman didn't hear me or if he didn't know that *Abrahamic* is the adjectival form of *Abraham*.

As my wife recounted the story, it made me think. There really is no covenant with Abraham in the Bible. In fact, there is no covenant with Noah or with David. There isn't even a covenant with Adam. I realized that every time God made a covenant, it was always "with you and your seed." God makes covenants with families, not individuals.

Please don't misunderstand. I am not saying that every child of every person in covenant with God will go to heaven. The Bible, and sadly our own experience, give countless contrary examples. But all who are born into the covenant are still born into the covenant. If they do not trust in the work of Christ alone, they are covenant breakers. And that is an altogether different thing from never having been in covenant.

There is a great deal of misunderstanding regarding God's covenants with men in the modern church. To help us grasp the meaning of this important term we are often told that a covenant is like a contract. Contracts we understand.

We live in a time of contracts. We have employment contracts, purchasing contracts, all manner of contracts. And there are indeed similarities between a covenant and a contract. In both forms there are typically agreements by both sides to do something. Tiger Woods agrees to wear a certain kind of hat while playing golf, and the company that makes the hat agrees to pay him a great sum of money.

In the covenant of grace, we are required to trust in the finished work of Christ alone (and not, by the way, in our trust). God, in turn, has vowed to remember not our sins and to impute to us the righteousness of Christ, so that we inherit the reward he has earned.

Covenants and contracts also typically include sanctions against those who do not do as promised. If Tiger Woods plays golf in the wrong hat, the contract stipulates assorted penalties against him. If the hat company fails to send Tiger his checks, they will likewise come under a stiff financial penalty.

When God made covenant with the children of Israel at the end of Deuteronomy, he listed not only a host of promises, should they keep the covenant, but verse after verse of chilling judgments should they fail to keep the covenant: "But it shall come to pass, if you do not obey the voice of the LORD your God, to observe carefully all His commandments and His statutes which I command you today, that all these curses will come upon you and overtake you: Cursed shall you be in the city, and cursed shall you be in the country. Cursed shall be your basket and your kneading bowl. Cursed shall be the fruit of your body and the produce of your land, the increase of your cattle and the offspring of your flocks. Cursed shall you be when you come in, and cursed shall you be when you go out" (Deut. 28:15–19). Moses goes on, but you get the picture. Nothing but bad things will come upon the children of Israel if they disobey.

There are, however, some very significant differences between covenants and contracts. Perhaps the greatest is the very nature of the agreement. Suppose I want Tiger Woods to wear a hat I have designed. Suppose he is not already under contract to another hat company. I tell him that if he will wear my hat every time he plays golf, then I will pay him five dollars. I venture to guess he will turn me down. He might, however, make a counter offer, suggesting that I pay him one billion dollars. In either situation he or I can walk away. I cannot make him wear my hat for what I offered. He cannot make me pay him that much money. We might sit down at a table and begin to negotiate. We might succeed in reaching an agreement, and we might not.

Covenants are not negotiated like contracts. Covenants are not negotiated at all. Covenants, particularly those in the ancient Near East, all follow the same pattern. They begin with neither stipulations nor sanctions, but an introduction of one side in the equation. When God begins the Ten Commandments, he says, "I am the LORD your God, who brought you out of the land of Egypt, out of the house of bondage" (Exod. 20:2). Why is that there? God is introducing himself as the sovereign one in the relationship. Ancient Near Eastern covenants are typically called "Suzerain-vassal treaties." The suzerain is the sovereign one, the one holding the power. The vassal is the servant. He does not negotiate with the suzerain, but accepts whatever conditions the suzerain lays down. In the Ten Commandments God affirms that he is laying down these commandments. There will be no negotiating.

This is an important distinction. To be sure, the covenants of God, even what some call the covenant of works with Adam, are filled with grace. That God imposes them is not an argument that they are in any way unfair. They all overflow with grace. But as we are grateful for God's grace, we must remember it is grace. We must remember that he has every right to impose this covenant on us. He does not ask our opinion on the matter. He does not ask if we want to be in covenant with him. He makes an offer we cannot refuse.

That is hard to swallow in our egalitarian and individualistic age. Our notion of fairness requires that we be allowed to negotiate, that we be able to opt out. We don't like the idea of the covenant being imposed on us. We don't like anything imposed on us, much less a series of obligations and then a series of punishments for failing to meet those obligations. Our preference notwithstanding, the covenant is imposed on us. Wishing things were different won't make it so. If we were wise, we would adjust our thinking to the way God operates, rather than pretending it's the other way around. It is wise to remember who is the suzerain and who is the vassal. It is wise to begin with the fear of God.

God promised Abraham a host of blessings. He said Abraham and Sarah, even in their old age, would bear a son. God promised that Abraham would be the father of many nations. He promised to Abraham the Promised Land. He promised that through Abraham all nations of the earth would be blessed. And most importantly, he promised to be God to Abraham. Remember, however, that the promise was to Abraham and his seed. The inheritance of the promise is an important part of the stories in Genesis about the patriarchs.

Abraham's impatience and disobedience led him to sire

Ishmael by Hagar. When he learned that Isaac was the promised son, there was the fear and then the faith that Abraham showed at Mount Moriah. Isaac bore two sons, Jacob and Esau, one of whom would inherit the promise and one of whom sold his birthright for a bowl of stew. Jacob's sons wrestled over who would have the position of prominence, leading them to betray the chosen one, Joseph. No one but God made these decisions, which culminated in his choosing Moses to lead the people out of Egypt.

Those covenants, or more properly that covenant, is still with us. Part of training my children is the constant singing of this song:

> Father Abraham had many sons.
> Many sons had Father Abraham.
> I am one of them, and so are you.
> So let's just praise the Lord.

I want my children to understand that they are not only my children, but also Abraham's children. They are not only in this same covenant, but are a part of the fulfillment of this covenant. Sprouls are not ethnically Jewish. Our ancestors are primarily Scots-Irish, which is why my children are named Darby, Campbell, Shannon, Delaney, and Erin Claire. But we are still the children of Abraham because the covenant promises that Abraham will be a blessing to the nations. When the gospel came to ancient Ireland, a part of that promise was fulfilled, and it continues to be fulfilled as it goes out to unreached people groups around the globe.

My people moved from Ireland to Scotland, and later back to Ireland. While they were in Scotland, the Reformation came. John Knox was persecuted and had to flee to Geneva. When he returned to Scotland, the first man he ordained was my direct ancestor, Robert C. Sproul. This decision, made centuries ago, is still reverberating through history and through my own life. It does not mean, of course, that all my paternal ancestors were pastors. It does not mean that each of them was a Presbyterian or even a Christian. But it does mean something. It places obligations on me.

That is what covenants made with families do to families. My son Campbell is actually Robert Campbell. He is the fifth consecutive generation in my family in which the first-born son is named Robert C. Bearing perhaps the greatest familial burden by virtue of my father's reputation, I thought carefully before my wife and I named our son. He will not suffer from the same comparisons with his father that I do with mine. He will be known in some circles as R. C. Sproul's grandson, which is not the same thing as being his son. I did, however, want to put a burden on him. That burden was not that he should write books or be on the radio or pastor a church, but that he should be a godly man. That's a part of the family catechism as well. Ask my son what he will be when he grows up, and he will tell you, "A godly man." He must be, because he is named for a series of godly men, my father, grandfather, great-grandfather, and that godly ancient Scotsman. My son cannot escape that duty. He can, of course, shirk it. But it is a duty nonetheless.

This is how God intended these things to happen. When God instructs the children of Israel in how to instruct their children, he tells them to teach their children the statutes and great deeds of God: "You shall teach them diligently to your children, and shall talk of them when you sit in your house, when you walk by the way, when you lie down, and when you rise up" (Deut. 6:7). Like the curses in chapter 28, this Hebrew idiom does not limit when parents are to teach these things, but communicates that this is a constant process—all day, every day.

Too many of us are not keeping covenant in this way. We treat the Christian faith the way we treat consumer goods. We treat our children like little adults. We communicate to them the benefits of the Christian faith. We tell them how pleased we are to be Christians. And then we wait and hope they will make the same choice. We don't want to force anything on them because, well, that's not the American way. It is, however, the biblical way. Paul commands us to bring up our children "in the training and admonition of the Lord" (Eph. 6:4). Ultimately our children are neither their own nor ours. They belong to God. And he commands us to raise them for him.

Paul, in his Letter to the Ephesians, also makes clear another relationship between covenants and families: not only does God make covenants with families, but also families make covenants between themselves. Families are a series of horizontal covenants in vertical covenant with God. There is a covenant between husband and wife, in which the wife is called to submit to her husband's authority over her. Paul says: "Wives, submit to your own husbands, as to the Lord. For the husband is head of the wife, as also Christ is head of the church; and He is the Savior of the body. Therefore, just as the church is subject to Christ, so let the wives be to their own husbands in everything" (Eph. 5:22–24). That, of course, is not a popular truth in our day. We have become so egalitarian that we assume that when one party must submit to another, the one submitting must be inferior to the other. This does not follow.

The first covenant that covenant theologians speak about is called the covenant of redemption. This covenant is not between God and man, whereby we have peace with God. Rather it is between the persons of the Trinity, made before all time. The Father, who ordains whatsoever comes to pass, elects the bride for his Son. The Son is sent by the Father to secure that bride, the church, through his incarnation, life, death, and resurrection. The Holy Spirit applies the Son's work in the lives of the elect, granting life through regeneration and working with the redeemed in their sanctification. The Son proceeds from, and is submissive to, the Father. The Spirit proceeds from the Father and the Son and is submissive to both. Yet all three persons are equal in substance, power, and glory. They have equal value but different roles. It does not follow that the one who submits is less valuable, less able, or less anything than the one to whom he or she submits.

While that truth may comfort us, strictly speaking it is unnecessary. Even if submission meant that the one who submits is in some respect less than the one to whom he or she submits, it would still be so. We may not like what God ordains here in Paul's epistle, but we are all under God's authority. To break the horizontal covenant here, the one established by God, is to break the vertical covenant.

In the horizontal covenant husbands have this duty: "Husbands, love your wives, just as Christ also loved the church and gave Himself for it" (Eph. 5:25). Another way we seek to undermine the wife's responsibility to submit to her husband is by emphasizing the great burden God, through Paul, places here on her husband. Sometimes women grumble that they would be delighted to submit to their husbands if their husbands were like Jesus. We're not. But here we are called to be just like Jesus. That's a burden.

Too often we seek to get out from under this burden by reducing it to something manageable. We tell our wives, "Dear, if ever we are walking through Central Park in New York City, and if, as it begins to get dark, some bad guy with a gun jumps out from behind a bush, I want you to know, dear, that I would step in front of you and take the bullet so that you could escape. Just like Christ loves the church, I love you enough to give myself for you."

But that is neither all that Christ does for the church nor all that Paul commands husbands to do. In this passage Paul goes on to say this: ". . . that He might sanctify and cleanse it [the church] with the washing of water by the word, that He might present it to Himself a glorious church, not having spot or wrinkle or any such thing, but that it should be holy and without blemish" (Eph. 5:26–27). That is sacrificial love. Husbands have a solemn, covenantal duty to sanctify their wives. The focus of the husband is not himself nor his work. His consuming passion is to be the holiness of his wife.

This brings us back to the very first covenant between God and man. We must remember that God's covenants are eternal. He does not change, and when he makes a covenant with our ancestor, he makes a covenant with us. From the very beginning of man, man was in covenant with God. "Then God said, 'Let Us make man in Our image, according to Our likeness; let them have dominion over the fish of the sea, over the birds of the air, and over the cattle, over all the earth and over every creeping thing that creeps on the earth.' So God created man in His own image; in the image of God

He created him; male and female He created them. Then God blessed them, and God said to them, 'Be fruitful and multiply; fill the earth and subdue it; have dominion over the fish of the sea, over the birds of the air, and over every living thing that moves on the earth'" (Gen. 1:26–28).

Perhaps one reason we are so beguiled by the world's thinking when it comes to the family is that we don't understand exactly what the family is for. The family exists to fulfill the dominion mandate first given to our Father Adam and Mother Eve. We know that chapter 2 of Genesis gives us a more detailed account of God's creation of Eve. He pronounces his first malediction not when the serpent arrives, but when he says, "It is not good that man should be alone" (Gen. 2:18a). Eve is God's solution, as God creates for Adam "a helper comparable to him" (2:18b).

A helper for what purpose? Did God create Eve to alleviate Adam's loneliness? Did God create Eve as a sort of playmate for Adam? God created Eve to help Adam exercise dominion over creation, bringing all things into submission. Marriage was not first for the joy that it brings, though it can do that. Marriage is not first for the romance, passion, and intimacy, though it can serve all these. Marriage is about dominion.

That is the covenant we are under. This covenant brings with it all manner of blessings when we obey. But when we treat the covenant as a means to blessing, we miss what we are called to do. It is only as we obey God's call on our lives, the stipulations of the covenant he imposes on us, that we experience this joy.

Beside me as I write, my dear wife, who is pregnant, is eating ice chips. It's not something she does every day. It is, however, something she does at the onset of labor. We are awaiting the arrival of our fifth blessing. We bear God's covenant children in obedience to that command to our parents that we be fruitful and multiply. We raise these children as the center of the garden we have been given to cultivate, seeking by his grace to raise them in the training and admonition of the Lord. We are teaching them that this is what God has called them to do, to raise up godly seed to exercise dominion over God's creation.

Soon—we hope very soon—the labor will become more difficult. When it is finished, however, we will rejoice in God's sight. We will see that just as he blessed Father Adam and Mother Eve, so has he blessed us. Just as he blessed Father Abraham and Mother Sarah, so has he blessed us. And we will look forward to the day when he will likewise bless our fruit with fruit of their own. When the labor is over we will cry tears of joy, as we receive from our heavenly Father this great reward. We will see, as always, that obedience in his covenants is its own reward, and that he, the true Lord of the Garden, faithfully crowns his own rewards with joy.

PART 1

———— ∞∞∞ ————

FATHERS

———— ∞∞∞ ————

*D*arby was just here in my office. She is my two-year-old
daughter. Darby is an Irish name which means "free
man." Those who know me well were not surprised that
freedom would have a prominent place in the name of my daughter
(nor that my Irish ancestry would be well represented). I have a
deep love of liberty. But why "man"? Those who know me also
know that I appreciate the virtues of masculinity and femininity and
that I don't like them blurred. So how did "man" get in my daughter's name? She is all girl. She walked about the office in her pink
t-shirt and pink bow doling out hugs like a congressman spending
money.

The question betrays the influence of American individualism.
Historically names sometimes bespoke not the named but others.
Isaac, Hebrew for "laughter," was named not for his own humor
but the skeptical laughter of his mother Sarah. Though I pray she
will one day marry one, Darby is by no means a free man. The
free man of which the name speaks is me.

Such a notion is hard to swallow in our particular culture.
Our idea of freedom evokes more of the Lone Ranger than a father
who knows best. Children, so it would seem, rob us fathers of our
money, our sleep, our time. The very dependence of children requires
that the father give up his independence. So whence my freedom?

As is so often the case, when we live coram Deo, before the
face of God, the thinking of the world gets turned upside down. My

freedom consists in large part in being free of the lies of the culture, in believing God's truth when all around me stumble in the darkness. I need not believe that children are a burden nor that my headship in my home is a heinous crime against equality. I need believe neither that manliness consists of owning a powerful truck, nor that manliness is having the power to blubber like a baby. Because God the Father has adopted me as his son, I am no longer a slave to folly. Because I am free, I no longer believe the lies of my former father, the father of lies. Because the shackles have been loosed and the blinders removed, I know I need to fear no man, but God alone. Our Captain and King has freed us so that we might be free men, and such are men indeed.

CHAPTER 1

⎯⎯∞∞∞⎯⎯

OUR STRONG
FATHER

⎯⎯∞∞∞⎯⎯

R. C. SPROUL

My son is the editor of *Tabletalk* magazine. Each month he gives me a sheet of written instructions for my article. He is a tough taskmaster, not unlike Pharaoh, who is loathe to give me straw for my quota of bricks. This month's instructions included this comment: "I'd hate to have to write on the frustrations of having your father work for you reluctantly. You need to be more zealous for these articles than I ever was about tending your yard."

His reference to my yard was provoked by a comment I made to him recently. My son now owns his own home. I noticed that he is inordinately fussy, indeed punctilious, about the care he gives his yard. I said to him, "Why didn't you give this kind of tender-loving-care to my yard when you used to cut the grass as a boy? I guess things change when you're tending your own yard rather than someone else's. It must be pride of ownership." So now it's turnabout and fair play.

I write my articles and books in the men's locker room at the club where I play golf. I have four lockers, one for my golf gear and three for my books. It is nice to have a not-so-quiet place where I have a constant supply of iced tea and a huge table to spread out my stuff and work. I am deaf to the rowdy by-play that goes on around me, even though it is often directed at me.

I live in two different worlds: the world of church and kingdom, and the secular world that finds its microcosm in the men's locker room. It is an exercise in contrast, yet one in which I find heartening intrusions of grace, where the distinctions between sacred and profane are sometimes blurred.

I love the guys who are denizens of the locker room. They are men in every sense of the word, and this place is their sanctuary. There is "Big Al," with his ponytail, his gruff voice, and a perpetual twinkle in his eye; "Rifle," the Polish golfer who endures endless ethnic jokes; "Fultie," the South African "bull" who is a regular on the PGA tour; "The Buck" (a.k.a. "Wild Bill"), the former NFL player; and a host of others, including "Tommy," "Fearless," "Pudge," "Chuckles," "X" (whose name is really Malcombe), "John," "Pat," "Doc," and "Guy." Guy is incorrigible. His favorite pastime is teasing R. C. Then there is Lee, who erupts every time I walk in the room. He raises his hands over his head and shouts, "Praise the Lord," and likens me to Benny Hinn. Lee's nickname is "Home Doggy" (figure that one out).

The locker room is the quintessential arena for male bonding. It is the place where "Skippers" and the boys all call each other "pards." Every day golf games are made, bets are arranged by strokes, first-tee arguments are settled, and Ron, when he lays his cards on the table for gin, shouts, "Call Rangoon!" The locker room/grill is off limits to women. It is a feminist's worst nightmare. It is a place of refuge where men are men, with all that this means, good and bad. It is a place for hard drinking and cursing, where men act like kids and are as rowdy as sailors on shore leave. It is also the place the guys refer to as "R. C.'s office," a term they use when answering the phone in the corner.

Recently I walked into this place after being on the road for three weeks. Things were strangely quiet as the guys were absorbed in card games. Doc Albert looked up and saw me enter. In a sing-song voice he loudly declared, "He's back!" After a perfectly timed Jack Bennyesque pause, he added in the same cadence, "Who cares?"

This is how I am treated in this place. I love every minute of it. These men tease me to death. The call me "Preacher" and make me the butt of a thousand jokes. They squirt me with water pistols while I'm writing and dump ice down my shirt if I turn my back. Yet I know they do care. And several of them come regularly to a weekly Bible study I teach, which was started at their request.

Men long for the love of a woman. But what they are sheepish to admit is that they also long for the love and concern of other comrades. Most of them are fathers. All of them are sons. All want the caring love of their fathers; not all received it. All wanted it and needed it; but all didn't get it.

I was one of the fortunate ones. No man ever displayed more care and affection for me than my father did. Like most boys, I embraced my father as my first and greatest hero.

Though he left this world almost forty years ago (Oops, Pudge just walked by and hollered, "What's happening, Rev?"), I have vivid memories of him and evoke them frequently. These memories are a rich legacy that endures.

One such memory jumps to mind. I had just returned from playing baseball. As I approached our driveway, still in uniform, lugging my bat over my shoulder with my spikes and glove dangling from the end of the bat, my next-door neighbor, Mr. Davies, called, "Did you win, Kiner?" I lit up inside, smiled, and said, "Yes, we won." I loved it that he always called me "Kiner," a reference to Pittsburgh's legendary homerun king, Ralph Kiner.

I proceeded down my driveway, where my father was standing by our backyard barbecue pit. Thick, juicy steaks sizzled on the grill. Dad said, "How'd you do?"

I said, "Great, Dad, I went three for four, two singles and a double."

He replied, "What did you do the other time?"

"I struck out."

With a mock frown he said, "Struck out! Then no steak for you for dinner."

I knew he was kidding. I knew he was really pleased, but it was his way to remind me that I still had lots of room for improvement. I knew that he cared. When he died a couple of years later, my world fell apart. My anger raged against God for taking my father from me. Not until I became a Christian was this rage supplanted by love and delight in my heavenly Father. Many people have trouble relating to God as Father. Their earthly fathers were so abusive and uncaring that they flinch when they hear God referred to as Father. This is not my problem. Though even God cannot completely fill the

hollow place left in my soul by the absence of my earthly father, God fills in me a greater void than the world's greatest
earthly father could ever fill.

God is the supreme Father of care. He loves, chastens, re-
bukes, corrects, disciplines, and instructs. But above all, he
cares. I take umbrage at those who, in their zeal for "political
correctness," seek to strip the Bible of its masculine imagery
and produce a version of gender-neutral language. This does
grave insult to the Holy Spirit, who, without a view toward
P.C. language, was pleased to inspire language drawn from
fallen humanity, both male and female, language that is ade-
quate to communicate the character of God.

Whatever else I may be, I am a man. I was born male, and
maleness is part of my identity, just as femaleness is part of
my wife's personal identity. That God is my Father means he
cares for me, that when I ask for bread I will not receive a
stone or a scorpion. His arms are strong. He is mighty in battle, a strong fortress for my soul. These terms may be masculine, but they are images of a strength that is tempered by
tenderness, virtues every child, boy or girl, long for in their
earthly father.

CHAPTER 2

⸻⸻

THE FATHER
AS PROPHET

⸻⸻

FRANKLIN SANDERS

L ike Paul, Christ called me to his service as a man already grown, as "one born out of due time" (1 Cor. 15:8). Imagine, then, my eerie astonishment a short time later when I discovered that with his last breath, my grandfather of seven generations removed had declared in 1767 the might and mercy of God. Humbled and surprised, I found I had inherited the duty of a prophet. God himself had ordained me to it before the foundations of the world, that he might glorify himself by his covenant faithfulness. This same office is the heritage of every Christian father.

As Americans we also inherit a handicap. With our mother's milk we drink in antibiblical notions of atomistic individualism, which cripple the performance of our duties as fathers. But we are not isolated servants of God, serving only ourselves and our children. We are one link in a *covenantal* chain of grace that reaches back to our first parent and forward through our children and grandchildren for thousands of generations (Exod. 20:5–6).

What do the Scriptures teach about the prophet? First of all, the word of God is in his mouth—the true Word, the sweet savor of Christ-like honey from a honeycomb. The prophet's office is not optional: God imposes it on us as a duty. The prophetic word also leads inevitably to active judgment. Therefore we must not only *speak* the Word, but also live and act it out.

The prophet's word is not just *any* word. It is not "wise tips for living" conjured up for our children out of our own experience. Our words must repeat the Word of God, revealed by his Spirit in the Scriptures.

That Word, living and active and sharper than any two-edged sword, also judges. The power of Christ's Spirit makes it effectual to genuine and eternal judgment.

Thus Christian fathers must discipline their children, but always according to the Word alone. The father as prophet declares the Word of God, teaches it to his children, then judges according to it. Your child learns the character, law, and mercy of God as you act it out in his life.

When you discipline, ask the child what he has done, declare the law, and then judge his act according to the law. "What did you do?"

"I went outside after Mama told me not to."

"What does the Bible say about obeying your Mama?"

"I am supposed to honor my mother and father."

"Did you honor your Mama when you disobeyed her?"

"No."

Then comes the punishment, *and then*, since the

prophet's goal is to bring the wayward to the mercy of God, comes repentance expressed and forgiveness granted.

God himself ordains the prophet's office, setting us aside before we are formed in the womb, so it is *not optional* to us. From Moses to Isaiah, when God calls prophets, they uniformly protest their lack of training, ability, and holiness, while God uniformly promises to supply whatever they need.

"By their fruits you shall know them," Christ says. Watchful children judge our word by our work. Thanks be to God, our children partake of God's forgiveness toward our manifold failures. When we sin against them, against our wives, or against others, we must be quick to repent and ask pardon, so that even out of our stumbling our Christian example may bring redemption.

But children can easily distinguish the faithful Christian from the hypocrite who mouths a standard of Christian obedience he will not follow himself. They filter every word through the grid of your example, both inside and outside the family.

Knowing that sin darkens our understanding, God not only gave us his written Word, but surrounds us also with *pictures* of himself, instructing our hearts, minds, and wills through our senses. "The heavens declare the glory of God" (Psalm 91:1).

Every time the church baptizes or celebrates the Lord's Supper, the grace and salvation of God in Christ are *pictured and acted out* before our eyes.

The prophet, too, pictures the Word of God in his own life, bringing a *heavenly* message by an *earthly* act. As the father serves his family as a prophet, so too this prophet serves church and commonwealth as a father, lovingly calling the wayward to obedience. The prophet acts out the Word and, like the faithful witness of Christ, also suffers for the Word.

Over and over God commands his prophets to act out his judgment on the nation and to picture before their eyes his mercy on Israel and all mankind. Again and again apostate church and state reward the prophets' faithful witness with beatings, imprisonment, and death.

In their own suffering the prophets show forth the faithful witness of obedience. To believer and unbeliever alike, what could more plainly reveal God's eternal power and enabling grace than the three Hebrew children in Nebuchadnezzar's fiery furnace? Or Daniel unharmed in the lion's den?

Because the rebellious world hates the Word, it also hates the Word-bearer. As Christ our Head suffered for the truth, so we also, prophets to our families, must be willing to "fill up whatever is lacking in Christ's sufferings." To be identified with him is to share his sufferings in history.

". . . others were tortured, not accepting deliverance, that they might obtain a better resurrection. Still others had trial of mockings and scourgings, yes, and of chains and imprisonment. They were stoned, they were sawn in two, were tempted, were slain with the sword. They wandered about in sheepskins and goatskins, being destitute, afflicted, tormented—of whom the world was not worthy. They wandered in deserts and mountains, in dens and caves of the earth" (Heb. 11:35b–38).

Like the prophets of old, we want to make alibis. We tell ourselves that today God's prophets are not called to such suffering. *Count the cost*, Jesus still says. "Whoever of you does not forsake all that he has cannot be My disciple" (Luke 14:33). The world still hates the Word, and if we as fathers and prophets do not faithfully "reveal the will of God for our salvation" by our works, then our words will fall fruitless to the ground.

But who is able to do such works? No one. But by the grace of God he promised to equip every man—to reveal through us in family, church, and state his will for our salvation, "through the blood of the everlasting covenant, . . . through Jesus Christ, to whom be glory forever and ever. Amen" (Hebrews 13:20–21).

CHAPTER 3

THE FATHER
AS PRIEST

MICHAEL S. BEATES

I am a product of our age. Like most twentieth-century men—no, like most men since Adam—I love leisure and too willingly abdicate my responsibility as father and husband to pursue it. Nowhere has the abandonment of God-given roles been more complete than in the area of father as priest.

I am haunted by the comments of James Alexander, who, nearly 150 years ago, wrote: "Our church cannot compare [regarding domestic worship] with that of the seventeenth century. Along with the Sabbath observance, and the catechizing of children, Family-Worship has lost ground. There are many heads of families, communicants in our churches, and (according to a scarcely credible report) some ruling elders and deacons, who maintain no stated daily service of God in their dwelling" (*Thoughts on Family Worship*). Saying we have lost ground understates to a frightening extent today's reality. Do you know *any* heads of families who faithfully conduct daily worship in the home?

I write not as one who has achieved success in the fatherly role of priest, but as one who, longing to fulfill that role, admits destitute failure. But in comparison to the chaotic and disintegrating social structures around us, I am easily persuaded that I am doing well merely by praying with my family before meals and at bedtime. After all, divorce reigns so common it no longer even surprises Christians.

Many loathsome men reject the priestly role by leaving the wives and children of their youth to spend their later years enjoying the pleasures of younger women. (More pitiable than loathsome are those men who reject their God-given priestly role, choosing instead to live in sexual union with other men.) Of marriages that survive, many suffer in silent ambivalence or in hidden betrayal. The "full quiver" of children is considered a liability to be avoided (or at least limited), not a blessing to be sought and nurtured. In such a climate, I easily think: "I am not so bad, really. Look at the rest of society."

Though usually better family-priests than the culture at large, believing men use several excuses for shirking the difficult and intimidating task of priestly care of their families. Many Christian men retreat to the safety of the hunter-gatherer-provider role. They claim the constraints of their work exempt them from priestly leadership. "If we want to live in this neighborhood and drive luxury cars," the husband says, "I must put in ten- to twelve-hour days and be on the road."

Though this excuse seems respectable, by defaulting his God-given role, the husband leaves spiritual oversight to his wife, who, with her nurturing nature, is only too ready to assume the forsaken duty.

Other men are quick to admit they feel ill-equipped, lacking knowledge of God's Word, having come to faith at an older age. Finally, many say it is simply too difficult to begin an ambitious task of overt leadership after years of prohibitive and competing routine.

Many believing men, handicapped by an upbringing devoid of a model of the father as priest, must first learn what a priest does in order to begin to fulfill such a role. A priest is one who mediates. When the law came, it exposed sin but was powerless to cleanse that sin. Being stained by sin, we need a mediator (a priest) to effect cleansing and renewal. The law is holy, just, and good, marking the way to life. Because people by nature are not holy, just, and good, that which was meant to bring life brought death instead. The priest intercedes redemptively between the holy God and the sinful people who need restoration.

God ordained the family as the basic social unit, a microcosm of society. A father, as head of this unit, carries responsibility for going before God to intercede for his family, and having done so, to lead his family to God in worship. Though difficult and demanding, this task (by God's grace) yields eternal, spiritual, and relational rewards against which earthly material gain cannot be compared.

The best examples of believers practicing consistently this godly form of family life are the English and American Puritans. J. I. Packer (in *A Quest for Godliness*) wrote, "The Puritan pastor, unlike his modern counterpart, did not scheme to reach the men through the women and children, but vice versa." For the Puritans, he said, the husband was the family pastor, responsible for channeling the family into religion, taking them to church, catechizing the children, teaching them the faith, examining the family after the sermon to check retention and understanding, filling any gaps along the way, leading family worship (ideally twice each day), and setting a godly example in all manners of living. John Geree, in a 1646 Puritan tract, said, "His family he endeavored to make a Church, . . . laboring that those that were born in it, might be born again to God." *The Geneva Bible* (1560) commented on Genesis 17:23, "Masters in their houses ought to be preachers to their families, that from the highest to the lowest they may obey the will of God."

Of course, the father's priestly duty is not restricted to certain times at home. Deuteronomy 4:9 and 6:4–9 remind us that the fathers must mediate the truth of God to their children, not only during "official" times of family worship, but in the course of everyday events, through the mundane, capturing the special, teachable moments with their children. John Angell James, in *The Christian Father's Present to His Children*, said, "The man who does not make the religious character of his children the supreme end of all his conduct toward them may profess to believe as a Christian, but certainly acts as an atheist."

Studies show that many fathers spend less than sixty seconds each day one-on-one with their young children. Think of the impact of beginning and ending each day with the father reading Scripture to the family and praying for the needs of his children. Consider the value of daily bringing before the family the Word of God, which quickens the spirit and pierces the conscience. When parents struggle to reach their children, they too often forget the best instrument through which to reach them—the Word.

Amid hectic schedules and frazzled lifestyles, daily worship allows the father to keep short accounts in the family. Arguments or disagreements cannot long remain unresolved when the family joins daily to hear the Scriptures read and commented on. "It sounds great," you say, "but with my family's schedule and activities it is simply not realistic." It is not realistic only because we have chosen to make other things more important. We have allowed the temporal and the cheap to rank above the eternal and the priceless. And believe me, these words convict and sting me as much as (I hope) they do you.

Though a father shoulders the burden of priesthood in the family, performing this task will unavoidably take him further in his own spiritual journey. The teacher always learns more than the student by virtue of preparation. When a father leads others to the throne of God in worship and speaks to the family from the Word of God, he must have spent time alone with God and time in God's Word, in order to then minister to his family.

James Alexander said, "Let other heirlooms perish, but let us not deny to our offspring the worship of that God who has been 'our dwelling-place in all generations.'" Like it or not, this is a man's job.

———— ❧❧❧ ————

CHAPTER 4

THE FATHER AS KING

———— ❧❧❧ ————

JUDY ROGERS

If we believe the familiar adage "A man's home is his castle," then what does that make the man? "KING!" many men would loudly respond, with beer steins lifted high in a toast to their tyrannical rule over the "subjects" in their domain. Others might timidly answer with a question, "King?" having abdicated any real position of leadership and assumed the role of a slave (in the word's most negative sense). Still others would laugh and appear quite content with being the "court jester," the "King of Fun" who "goes along to get along," as his wife (or ex-wife) and children squander the family treasury and make all the decisions. So is a man KING in his "castle"? Indeed! But who gives him this authority and what kind of king should he be?

God himself gave man not only the right but the responsibility to be king. He created man in his image to be his vice-regent with dominion over the creatures. God also made Eve in his image to be the queen of creation and a helpmeet to Adam. But because of God's created order of submission—Christ to God, man to Christ, and woman to man (1 Cor. 11:3; Eph. 5:23), Adam was the God-ordained head of Eve.

In his book *Man and Woman in Christian Perspective*, Werner Neuer says this regarding 1 Corinthians 11:3: "It does not say 'the husband should be the head of the wife' but the husband 'is the head of the wife as Christ is the head of the church.' The husband is therefore placed over his wife constitutionally. . . . Just as one cannot confess Jesus Christ without affirming his lordship, so it is impossible to confess maleness without affirming male headship." His kingship as head of his home, then, is not a position of greater worth than his wife's (Gal. 3:27–28), but a fulfilling of his constituted role.

How should we understand the kingly role of husbands and fathers? Even in the church of the Lord Jesus Christ, we find too many men who, for one reason or another, have lost their footing in the biblical world of manhood and fail to emulate Christ in his role as King. No doubt most Christian men would zealously agree that we are to "be like Jesus," to "follow His steps" (1 Peter 2:21), and yes, even go so far as to ask that soul-searching question, "What would Jesus do?" What, indeed, did Jesus do (and what does he continue to do) as King, and how can husbands and fathers follow in his steps?

I have composed songs for many of the *Westminster Shorter Catechism's* questions. These songs help us to understand more practically these biblical principles and to hide God's Word in our hearts. In the song "Jesus Our Prophet, Priest, and King", we sing the following:

> Jesus our King is exalted above,
> He rules and defends all His people in love,
> He fights all our battles . . . In Him we are free,
> And He will destroy His and our enemies!

Jesus is exalted as King of Kings! Ephesians says, ". . . according to the working of His mighty power which He worked in Christ when He raised Him from the dead and seated Him at His right hand in the heavenly places, far above all principality and power and might and dominion, and every name that is named, not only in this age but also in that which is to come" (Eph. 1:19–21). Imagine such a high and mighty position! But how did he get there? The great King of Kings was exalted because he first humbled himself to servanthood, as we see in Philippians: ". . . [Christ Jesus] made Himself of no reputation, taking the form of a servant, and coming in the likeness of men. And being found in appearance as a man, He humbled Himself and became obedient to the point of death, even the death of the cross. Therefore God also has highly exalted Him and given Him the name which is above every name. . . ." (Phil. 2:7–9). Many a man may read with new eyes Ephesians 5:22 ("Wives, submit to your own husbands") when they grasp once and for all what this great and humble King did for his glorious, though imperfect, bride.

Werner Neuer gives us clear insight into this matter: "Without the comparison of Christ, the primacy of [submission to] the husband 'in everything' (Eph. 5:24) could be misunderstood as a license for every form of male tyranny. The comparison with Christ shows the content, character, and limits of this subjection. Christ's headship is a reign of sacrificial love" (*Man and Woman*).

Who would not desire such a husband and father to reign in their midst and defend them? Yet many men today grievously fail to understand loving headship. When a man comprehends that he is not to "lord it over" his family but to submit humbly to his Lord, he will be ready to execute all the duties and privileges of one called by God to such a weighty position. Following are two "fleshed out" examples of representative kingship from my experience, my father and my husband.

My father, C. C. Belcher, presented a wonderful picture of the kingship of Christ. He protected me from my indwelling sin by refusing to give in to my childish and selfish whims. When I disobeyed, he "subdued me to himself" through firm but loving discipline (I often had to break my own "switch" from a nearby tree). I still recall my tears that flowed from my eyes as I looked on his grieved countenance; but upon my confession and repentance, he quickly forgave me and our close relationship was restored. How beautifully he mirrored the kingly aspects of Christ! Oh, for every little girl to have such a father!

My husband, Wayne, demonstrates Christ-like kingship in our home by setting forth godly principles in a dominion-oriented context, directives that are followed (though imperfectly) by the entire family. He rules, not like a cold, unapproachable dictator, but like a wise leader who takes time to weigh carefully each matter. He understands that loving rule seeks to base decisions on clear, biblical principles that will please God, rather than sacrifices truth for a season of super-ficial "peace."

He seeks to defend us against our spiritual enemies by diligently studying the Word, thereby discerning which teachings and influences are trustworthy and appropriate and which would harm our family's spiritual well-being. Involve-ment in the political process to help elect godly leaders is also a vital aspect of his kingly defense. He protects us not only by providing a secure house and reliable cars, but also by being alert to our physical and emotional needs.

When I've had a trying day, he notices this and offers to take me out to dinner. Yet he carefully instructs me in areas in which my own attitudes or emotions may harm others or even me. He has protected both our daughters from the be-ginning. He protected them not only physically, but also emotionally. He instructed and trained them to consider only godly, like-minded men for husbands. He made sacrifices at times to accomplish this. He corrects and counsels our col-lege-age son like the father in Proverbs, challenging our son to consider his relationships and future calling, and seeking to protect him from as many evil and negative influences as possible.

He fights our battles by taking on trials that confront any of us, making every effort to exercise wisdom and execute jus-tice concerning matters within the family and battles outside of it. He would tell you that he has not done all of this with complete consistency or without error, but we praise God that he has pictured for us the kingship of Christ.

Jesus at once displayed Godhood and manhood, power and humility, authority and submission, headship and ser-

vanthood. In the imperfect state of manhood, men can still, by
God's Spirit, display these same attributes, not equating manliness with a king-of-the-hill mentality, but humbly falling in
line behind the King of kings as "little kings." God calls a father to "not provoke your children to wrath, but bring them
up in the training and admonition of the Lord" (Eph. 6:4), and
a husband to love his wife "just as Christ also loved the church
and gave Himself for it" (Eph. 5:25). When he becomes a nurturing father and servant-husband, he will be qualified to rule
lovingly over his family as king—with a small "k."

PART 2

⟨⟨⟨⟩⟩⟩

MOTHERS

⟨⟨⟨⟩⟩⟩

I *have a friend who was recently married. When we met I was impressed with her character: I tend to be impressed with missionaries and their children. Being overseas in intemperate, hostile lands can do wonders for sheltering people from the far more dangerous and pernicious character-destroyers in America. She explained then that she had had several serious beaus, but that none of them had been right. I asked if these young men had been godly men. She answered with an emphatic yes, and so I took to calling her* GAGE, *an acronym for "Godly Ain't Good Enough." She is finally satisfied and so has married, having found her "Bo" (his real name). He is, she assures me, a godly young man.*

Sigmund Freud, though quite sure he had plumbed the contours of the psyche and unlocked the depths of the subconscious, still had to ask wistfully, "What do women want?" It is the far less learned but equally perplexed editor of Family Practice *who must conclude, "I don't know."*

Freud's humility is a step in the right direction. Today we have an army of experts equipped with their secular sheepskins to guide us through the murky waters of women's desires. We have organizations like the National Organization of (some) Women who proclaim to the world with shrill voices what women want. We even have special meetings of pseudo-governmental agencies like the recent Beijing conference to draw up a nice, neat list of women's demands.

The best answer to the question "What do women want?" is, "Wrong question." We ought to be far more concerned with what women need, or to put it another way, with what God wants for women. We need not then consult with professed experts, but must look to God's Book. He, of course, is the ultimate expert. After all, he made women.

Too often the church seems more interested in the advice of experts than the commands of the Expert. Living coram Deo, however, works differently. To live before the face of God is to affirm the right of our Husband in heaven to mold us into his image. For women, it is not so much to desire to be beautiful, successful, or powerful, but to recognize that to be godly is good enough, that it doesn't get any better than this.

CHAPTER 5

HOLY MOTHER
CHURCH

R. C. SPROUL

Historians are not certain who said it. The statement has been attributed by some to Cyprian, by others to Augustine. The assertion has survived since the early centuries of Christian history: "Who does not have the church as his mother does not have God as his Father." From its earliest days the church was given the appellation "Mother."

The use of paternal and maternal language is an intriguing phenomenon in religion. The pattern of comparative religion indicates a strong tendency among people to seek transcendent models in both male and female figures. The Greeks had both gods and goddesses in their pantheon. The Egyptians revered Isis, the wife of their ruling god. So the Greek goddess Hera corresponded to the Roman Juno. Mythological deities commonly include a queen as well as a king.

The role of Mary in Roman Catholic religion is significant. She reigns as the "Queen of Heaven" and is the Holy Mother to whom the faithful can go for solace. The recent gnostic apotheosis of "Sophia" provides a rallying point for the feminization of Christianity.

However we respond to these developments, we cannot deny the virtually universal tendency to seek ultimate consolation in some sort of divine maternity. We have all experienced the piercing poignancy that attends the plaintive cry of a child who, in the midst of sobs, says, "I want my mommy." Who of us when we were children never uttered these words? Who of us as parents has not heard these words? As a father I recall my own children sobbing them. I experienced no jealousy or sense of rejection when they cried for their mother. I could identify with them, remembering those words crossing my own lips. Nor is this cry restricted to children. It is a matter of record that soldiers who are wounded in battle and dying, often cry out for their mothers. When football players are caught in the eye of the TV camera, they rarely say, "Hi, Dad."

The Bible itself not only describes God in the masculine image of Father but also borrows from feminine imagery at times. Some scholars argue that the semitic, linguistic roots of the divine title *El Shaddai* referred to the "multibreasted one," the one who could provide the nation with succor and nourishment. Jesus himself, lamenting over Jerusalem, cried, "O Jerusalem, Jerusalem, the one who kills the prophets. . . . How often I wanted to gather your children together, as a hen gathers her chicks under her wings, but you were not willing!" (Matt. 23:37). The brooding of the Spirit over primordial waters (Gen. 1:2) conjures up a similar maternal image.

In the Bible the supreme feminine image is ascribed, not to a goddess or female consort of God, but to the church. Before the church is ever seen as a mother, she is first revealed as a bride. In the Old Testament the commonwealth of Israel is the bride of Yahweh; in the New Testament the church is the bride of Christ.

The resulting familial imagery is somewhat strange. God is Father; Christ is the Son. As the Son of God, Christ is then referred to as our Elder Brother. The church is his bride. In the language of family, this would then mean that the church is our sister-in-law. But who ever speaks of "holy sister-in-law church"? It is rare in family life that a younger sibling looks to his older brother's wife as an ersatz mother, though at times such a wife may exercise that role.

But we, both men and women, are given the title "Bride of Christ." I am male, yet I am part of a body that is described in feminine terms. What is more strange is that the same entity called a bride, of which I am a part, is regarded as my mother. I cannot be my own mother.

These images are not the result of a jumbled mass of confusion. It is not nonsense to refer to the church as our mother. Though born of the Spirit, we are birthed into spiritual life chiefly within the cradle of the church. If the church is not our birthplace, it is surely our nursery. In her bosom the means of grace are concentrated. The church nurtures us unto mature faith.

This nurturing function of the church most clearly links it to the maternal image. In the church we receive our spiritual food. We gain strength from the sacraments ministered to us. Through the Word we receive our consolation and the tears of broken hearts are wiped clean. When wounded, we go to the church for healing.

When someone asks, "Is the church an army or a hospital?" their question posits a false dilemma. It is both. It is an army, called to be the church militant. But no army worthy of the name shoots its own wounded. It is also a hospital, erected by Christ himself and entrusted with the care of wounded souls.

Though the church is *our mother*, it is also *Christ's bride*. In this role we are the object of Christ's affections. Corporately we are his beloved. Stained and wrinkled, in ourselves we are anything but holy. When we say the church is holy or call her "holy mother church," we do so knowing that her holiness is not intrinsic. It is instead derived from and dependent on the one who sanctifies her and covers her with the cloak of his righteousness. As the sensitive husband shelters his wife and chivalrously lends her his coat when she is chilled, so we are clad from on high by a Husband who stops at nothing to defend, protect, and care for his betrothed. His is the ultimate chivalry, a chivalry that no upheaval of earthly custom can eradicate or make passé. This chivalry is not dead because it cannot die.

The bride of Christ is soiled, but she will one day be presented spotless to the Father by the Son who bought her, who loves her, and who intercedes for her every day. If we love Christ, we must love his church. For he who does not have the church as his mother does not have God as his Father.

CHAPTER 6

⸺∘⸺

THE WOMAN
AS WIFE

⸺∘⸺

EDNA GERSTNER

One of the most interesting speaking dates I ever had was when I was pushed into an emergency one while my husband was doing graduate work at Harvard. The group was called the Harvard Dames.

I was attending an afternoon meeting at which the poet Robert Frost was to speak. The program chairman grabbed me as I entered the auditorium. She was in a panic. Frost was not going to make it. She knew I spoke for church groups. Would I pinch hit for him?

So I talked about "Women in India." I told them about my father, a missionary in the Central Provinces (now Madhya Prodesh), coming home from an evangelistic tour through the thick jungles that surrounded our home when he heard the cry of an animal in pain. He had the tonga stop in order to put the animal out of its misery. To his surprise he found a little girl, about four years of age, sitting in a clearing eating grass. It was famine time, and no doubt her family had felt it necessary to rid itself of one mouth to feed. Her parents had left her there either to die of starvation or to be devoured by jungle animals. My mother told me this did not mean that the parents did not love the little girl. But if one child had to be sacrificed, it would of course be a daughter. The funeral pyre of the parents must be ignited by a son. If not, the deceased go to hell and their progeny with them. The Hindu word for *boy* is *putra*: *put* means "hell" and *ra*, "deliverer." We took that baby in and fed her milk with an eyedropper. She grew healthy and strong and was adopted by a Christian family who named her Dukne ("little sorrow"). She was my friend.

I was underlining to this predominately secular group how much we women owed to Christianity and to the biblical view that God's image is stamped on both sexes.

When women in the United States try to trace the subjugation of women to the Bible, I remember Dukne. When they are appalled by Ephesians 5:22, "Wives, submit to your own husbands, as to the Lord," I contrast it with a passage in the *Puranas*, one of the Hindus' sacred books: "Let a women who wishes to perform sacred oblations wash the feet of her lord and drink the water, for her husband is her lord, her priest, her religion. Wherefore abandoning all else she ought to chiefly worship her husband."

It is important to notice that although the Bible clearly instructs wives to be subordinate to their husbands, it limits the scope of obedience. In Colossians the wife is exhorted to obedience "as is fitting in the Lord" (Col. 3:18).

We all know the story of Vashti's godly "No." When her husband asked her to dance before a crowd of drunken guests, she refused. We may not think often about the godly Sarah telling a half-lie for her husband. She should never have passed herself off as her husband's sister. Even though it was true (she was his half-sister), it was misleading and therefore tantamount to a lie. As a result she almost landed in a harem and polluted the godly line of Abraham. The Bible is very clear. Obedience is required in normal circumstances, but only "as is fitting in the Lord." As Peter said when commanded to cease preaching, "We ought to obey God rather than men" (Acts 5:29).

We also tend to overlook, in our emphasis on Ephesians 5:22, the preceding verse, "submitting to one another in the fear of God" (5:21). Everyone must at times be submissive to others. Even in the home the Bible spells out clearly where the husband must be subject to his wife: "The wife does not have authority over her own body, but the husband does. And likewise the husband does not have authority over his own body, but the wife does" (1 Cor. 7:4).

If this is the case, why did God make man the head and not the woman? Some attempt to prove that man, per se, is better able to rule, overlooking women such as Elizabeth I, Indira Ghandi, and Golda Meir. But do such attempts really matter? The all-wise God planned it this way, and therefore it is best. No one can seriously opt for a "It's your turn to rule this time, honey; next time it will be mine."

We all can theorize about the "why." My own feeling is that God gave woman the edge, and this order of obedience is a balancing act.

How often we have heard, "The hand that rocks the cradle is the hand that rules the world." And I remember being practically knocked off my chair when, as a student at the University of Pennsylvania, I heard a professor champion the double standard in morality. "No man can be sure of his fatherhood," the professor argued. "At least, promiscuous as she may be, the woman can be certain that the child is hers." And that was in 1935!

For those women who are very independent, why not remain single? As such, you may serve the Lord much better and without chafing. But if you decide to enter into the state of matrimony, please add these questions to the many you will ask about the man you plan to marry: Will he be easy for me to obey? Do I trust his judgment? If you start out feeling wiser than he is, there will be rocks ahead.

Many, like me, would hate to be in charge with all the responsibilities it entails. If I were a husband, I would have to qualify under a verse in the Bible that scares me: "Likewise you husbands, dwell with them with understanding, giving honor to the wife, as to the weaker vessel, and as being heirs together of the grace of life, that your prayers may not be hindered" (1 Peter 3:7).

Dear Jesus, please make me a Christian wife! My husband must bear a heavy burden, and so I must pray.

CHAPTER 7

───❦───

THE WOMAN
AS MOTHER

───❦───

NANCY WILSON

otherhood is in a muddle. Christian women today
are hard-pressed to find a pattern of godly motherhood to emulate in popular culture. Although our
modern world espouses several views of motherhood, each is,
not surprisingly, seriously flawed.

One widely held notion is that motherhood is an inconvenience. It interrupts career plans and ruins the figure. It is
a royal and expensive nuisance. Obviously the abortion mill
is fueled in part by this attitude. But subtly Christian women
are not invulnerable to this viewpoint. They have heard it so
much that many agree with the world that children are "not
for everyone"—at least "not right now." Pursuit of career, financial independence, and leisure are given preeminence.

Motherhood is one of many options and is easily "put off." Thanks to modern scientific technology, babies can be arranged to fit in at a more convenient time. Thus women deny themselves.

The obvious extension of this view is the woman who has children but considers them an inconvenience. She dumps most of the burden of her children on school and daycare. She looks for ways to find her own space, because, our culture tells her, she deserves it. The result of this attitude can be seen in our supermarkets (e.g., public displays of annoyance) and on our streets, where lost and lonely adolescents are adrift with no sense of what a family is.

Many who in their twenties pursued careers, find themselves in their thirties or forties with an emptiness, a dissatisfaction, a hollowness, a lack of fulfillment. Despite their worldly success, an indefinable "longing" sets in. They begin to see motherhood as an "experience" they want. This attitude perceives motherhood as simply a personal accomplishment. "I have been a successful lawyer, so now I'd like to experience motherhood."

Children, however, are not a prize to win, a goal to achieve, or something to possess that will make our lives more meaningful or complete. "I've got the house, the cars, the vacation home, the career . . . now all I need is a couple of kids." Women who look at children as a means of personal fulfillment are mistaken at two points. First, experience satisfies only temporarily. It can never bring a lasting sense of fulfillment and purpose. Each passing experience reveals the need for another and better one. Second, this view is just another manifestation of self-centeredness and undervalues the purpose and significance of motherhood as God designed it.

A third view of motherhood stands in odd contrast to the children-are-an-imposition perspective, but is not far removed from the experience-oriented outlook. This is the sentimental, romantic view of motherhood. We see "cards for mother" by the truckload, decorated with hearts, bows, bunnies, and glitter on the outside and with trite verses on the inside. This reduces motherhood to an emotional state: babies are sweet, cute, and adorable, and they always love you.

This sentimentalism is dangerous. Any time our emotions drive the car, we soon end up in a ditch. Babies wake up in the night; they get sick; sometimes they even die. The tender, sweet, emotional side of motherhood is precious, but only because hardheaded reason and biblical discipline, with lots and lots of hard work, are steering the process.

Christian women need to have their perspective on mothering anchored in the Scriptures, not in modern culture. It is imperative that they know how the Bible defines mothering, for this protects them against the ungodly pressures to conform to the world. Christian women must learn to think like Christians about these things.

When a young woman marries, her identity changes radically. She is no longer a daughter, but a wife. Her name changes. She has a new head and new responsibilities as her husband's helper. Then when she becomes a mother, her body changes and with it often her emotions. A little person comes into the world who is completely dependent on her. All these changes require a biblical frame of reference to enable a woman to anticipate, understand, and appreciate who she is in God's world and what her responsibilities are as a wife and mother. Scripture illumines this for her and provides security in the midst of modern folly.

Good mothering is a learned skill. Titus 2:3–4 commissions older women to live holy lives so that they are fit to teach younger women "to love their husbands, to love their children." Christian women cannot learn mothering from talk-show hosts, magazine articles at the checkout stand, or classes on self-esteem. A healthy, godly view of mothering must be learned from the Scriptures. (For more on this, see chap. 8.)

Scripture teaches that being a mother is not automatically a blessing. Solomon says, "A wise son makes a glad father, but a foolish son is the grief of his mother" (Prov. 10:1). Being a mother can be, and often is, a grief. "A foolish son is a grief to his father, and bitterness to her who bore him" (Prov. 17:25). Raising children to righteousness, however, is a blessing. "The father of the righteous will greatly rejoice, and he who begets a wise child will delight in him. Let your father and your mother be glad, and let her who bore you rejoice" (Prov. 23:24–45).

A wise mother realizes she can have a tremendous impact for good on future generations through her children. Knowing that God desires "godly offspring" (Mal. 2:15), she faithfully teaches her children his ways. "My son, hear the instruction of your father, and do not forsake the law of your mother" (Prov. 1:8). Proverbs 31 is the result of the teaching of King Lemuel's mother, and her teaching continues to bless generations of believers. This kind of mother has her reward when "her children rise up and call her blessed" (Prov. 31:28). A Christian view of mothering calls for child-rearing to the glory of God.

Motherhood is not a romanticized ideal, but a God-given task suited to a woman's frame. This task is accomplished by

hard work through his grace and provision. Godly motherhood does not focus exclusively on infancy and childhood. It
also focuses on the long-term objective: spiritually mature
sons and daughters who live to bring honor and glory to God.
This is the calling of scriptural motherhood.

CHAPTER 8

A WOMAN'S
MANDATE

ELISABETH ELLIOT

When speaking to a group of pastors' wives, I learned that 80% of them worked full time outside the home. I was shocked.

Is it wrong for a pastor's wife—or any other wife—to have a job? Another question should be asked first: What has God said about women's work?

The consensus among Christians seems to be that careers for women are to be not only permitted but also encouraged. If we look carefully at the scriptural lists of womanly responsibilities (1 Tim. 5:9–10 and Titus 2:3–5), we may ask whether there is *time* to do those things that are clearly the will of God when we have set for ourselves so ambitious an agenda. Paul's letter to Timothy spells out which women qualify for the widows' list. First on the list of "good works" is *bringing up children.*

Who of us has not noticed—in airports, grocery stores, and at church suppers—the wild and uncontrolled children, racing and screaming, while parents stand helplessly by, rolling their eyes, shrugging their shoulders, and saying, "They're just kids—what can you do?" Bless their hearts, they do not know there is something they *can* do, because no one has taught them. But where, I ask, are the older women who could teach the younger? They don't seem to be at home anymore.

> In the dim and distant past
> When life's tempo wasn't fast,
> Grandma used to rock and knit,
> Crochet, tag, and babysit.
> Grandma now is at the gym
> Exercising to keep slim.
> Now she's golfing with the bunch,
> Taking clients out to lunch.
> She's going north to ski and curl,
> And all her days are in a whirl.
> Nothing seems to stop or block her
> Now that Grandma's off her rocker.
> —Source unknown

My own life has been blessed by having, first and foremost, a godly mother who was always *there.* She stayed home. She raised six children, and set for us a holy example of femininity, self-discipline, discipline (an 18-inch switch lay on the lintel of the door of every room in the house), humor, and love. I have also been greatly blessed by spiritual mothers—

older women who happened to be there geographically when my mother was not, women who had time for me. They would not have thought of themselves as spiritual mothers. They were simply being kind to a young woman who needed their example, their steadfastness, their godly counsel, their prayers.

I have called such women WOTTs: Women of Titus Two. Someone asked for guidelines, structure, organization, information about how to establish a WOTTs group in her church. God forbid that we start another organization; we do not need another *meeting*. But perhaps we could try this:

1. Pray. Ask God to show you what is needed and how you yourself can help. Pray with one or two others who understand the need and who do not balk at the sacrifice (perhaps on the phone if it's difficult to get together). The measure of our love is the measure of our willingness to be inconvenienced.

2. Ask your pastor if he will preach on the two crucial passages (1 Tim. 5:9–10 and Titus 2:3–5). If he consents, he's a man of uncommon courage.

3. In Bible studies, Sunday school classes, over your kitchen table, or wherever you have opportunity, raise the subject of spiritual mothering. Tell others of the blessing older, wiser, godlier women have been to you. If you have no such examples in the flesh, try finding them in a book. Amy Carmichael became one to me as I read her books. Her biography, *A Chance to Die*, has helped many.

4. Post a list on the church bulletin board of WOTTs—women who earnestly desire to be available and who are humble enough to be unsung. No one, of course, can promise to be available at all times or to meet all demands, but it would help younger women to know there are a few listening ears when they don't know what to do with an uncommunicative husband, a 25-pound turkey, or a two-year-old's tantrum.

It is doubtful that the Apostle Paul had in mind Bible classes or seminars or books when he spoke of *teaching* younger women. He meant the simple things, the everyday example, the willingness to take time from one's own concerns to pray with the anxious mother, to walk with her the way of the cross—with its tremendous demands of patience, selflessness, lovingkindness—and to show her, in the ordinariness of Monday through Saturday, how to keep a quiet heart.

These lessons will come perhaps most convincingly through rocking a baby, doing some mending, cooking a supper, or cleaning a refrigerator. Through such an example, one young woman—single or married, Christian or not—may glimpse the mystery of charity and the glory of womanhood, so perfectly exemplified in the response of a humble village girl of long ago when she said: "Behold the maidservant of the Lord! Let it be to me according to your word" (Luke 1:38).

PART 3

∞

CHILDREN

∞

*B*iblical analogies are like the chicken and the egg. When I make an analogy I connect some sort of abstract principle to a preexisting reality. If I say, "Life is like a hamburger," I am trying to explain something about this slippery thing, "life," by pointing to something we know all about, hamburgers. But when God makes analogies, it gets more difficult. We have to ask which came first, the analogy or the reality? Did God, for instance, create the institution of marriage to teach us something about how Christ relates to the church? Or did God use marriage to explain that relationship?

Do I learn how to relate to my earthly father by looking at my relationship to God? Or do I learn how to relate to God by looking at my relationship to my father? God's Word tells us that God is our father. That makes all of us children. My guess is that in understanding this biblical analogy we tend to see God in the light of our fathers. The thought that God is our father is apt to lead us into a fit of warm fuzzies. It all seems so warm and cozy. God, we think the Bible is telling us, is some celestial catch player or story reader. He hugs us when he comes home from work, and he fixes our broken toys. We tame God, turning him into a larger-than-life daddy-figure.

The Bible does teach that God is our father. And there is real comfort there. What we seem to miss is that this means we are God's children. Rather than diminish or demean God by bringing him low, this analogy should fill our chests with pride and lift us up. WE ARE HIS CHILDREN. Can you believe it? We share an identity. We are of the same family. I am, in some very real way, like him.

Of course only God is God. False religions teach that humans can become gods. We know that we cannot take on aseity, infinity, omnipotence. There is but one who is all that. And we are his children.

In union with Christ we become the children of God. Through his Son I became his son. As we look at children in part 3, remember whose children we are, and rejoice.

We live in his presence, coram Deo. We move beneath his paternal gaze. Though we see it only dimly now, one day we will see him clearly, and we shall, like sons and daughters, be like him.

CHAPTER 9

––––∞∞∞––––

COUNT THE
STARS

––––∞∞∞––––

R. C. SPROUL

A recent event changed my life forever. Indeed it changed not only my life but the lives of many people who are close to me. This event was the birth of a baby. Recently my son and daughter-in-law became the parents of a baby boy, whose name is Robert Campbell Sproul. Campbell, as he is called, represents the fifth generation of R. C. Sprouls. When he was born, I said to my son, "Now I have an heir." He replied: "Perhaps there is something you have forgotten, Dad. You already have an heir." My daughter would be quick to change that from *heir* to *heirs*.

My son was correct. Now I have another heir, another grandchild. The arrival of this new grandchild will change more than my last will and testament. It will change the entire dynamic of our family relationships.

When Campbell was being born, his two-year-old sister, Darby, stayed with my wife and me. After receiving word of Campbell's arrival, we told Darby that she had a new brother. She understood little of what that meant. As we traveled to the hospital with Darby, we tried to generate excitement about her new brother. When we arrived, Darby was more interested in the elevator than in Campbell. She didn't realize that her life would never be the same. Her family had suddenly changed. She was no longer an only child. My son and his wife would also experience a radical change in their lives. There is now another mouth to feed, another child to tutor, a son to love and embrace.

As our modern culture ceases to value families, we often hear talk of the crisis of "family values." I notice in this rhetoric a subtle equivocation in the meaning of the word *values*. The tendency is to use *values* as a synonym for *ethics*. But values and ethics are not the same thing. Ethics is concerned with norms, with objective standards of right and wrong. To be sure we live in an age in which ethics are relativized and reduced from norms to mere preferences. Perhaps this is why it has become so easy to use *values* and *ethics* as if they were identical.

Values have to do with preferences. They are subjective. The subjective theory of values declares that the value of goods and services is determined not by the cost of their production but by the worth attributed to them by those who do or do not desire them.

Because values are subjective and ethics are objective, we may leap to the conclusion that they are unrelated. But biblically speaking, a close connection exists between values and ethics. It is an ethical concern to bring our values into line with God's values. We ought to value our souls more than the goods of the whole world, our faith more than our reputation.

The crisis of family values begins with how we value people. The Bible views children as gifts from God that are of inestimable value. In the Old Testament a family with a "full quiver" of children is seen as a great blessing. Conversely barrenness is seen as a great calamity.

We see this vividly in the case of Abraham: ". . . the word of the LORD came to Abram in a vision, saying, 'Do not be afraid, Abram. I am your shield, your exceedingly great reward.' But Abram said, 'Lord GOD, what will You give me, seeing I go childless, and the heir of my house is Eliezer of Damascus?' Then Abram said, 'Look, You have given me no offspring; indeed one born in my house is my heir!' And behold, the word of the LORD came to him, saying, 'This one shall not be your heir, but one who will come from your own body shall be your heir.' Then He brought him outside and said, 'Look now toward heaven, and count the stars if you are able to number them.' And He said to him, 'So shall your descendants be'" (Gen. 15:1–5).

Abraham was one of the wealthiest men of the ancient world. His herds and flocks were huge. God appeared to him and declared that the Lord himself would be Abraham's great reward. Abraham's response borders on cynicism: "What will You give me, seeing I go childless?" This question reveals volumes about Abraham's values. Despite his riches he felt impoverished because he lacked children. His wife was barren. He had goats and sheep, but no descendants. He complained to God that his only heir was a servant who worked for him.

For Abraham the chief component of the patriarchal blessing he was promised (apart from redemption) was children and grandchildren. He was to receive a gift from his own loins that would be flesh of his flesh and bone of his bone. Throughout the Old Testament the abundance of children is seen as a manifold blessing from God, the lack of children as a great disaster. Somebody forgot to tell the people of God that the ideal family consists of a husband, a wife, and two children. They were not informed of the niceties of family values by Planned Parenthood.

Recently I was taping a radio broadcast. Six people in the studio audience indicated that they were from Pittsburgh, the city of my birth and childhood. I asked them where they had been born. They mentioned various hospitals in the Pittsburgh area, among them one that years ago enjoyed the reputation of being Pittsburgh's "baby hospital." Of course all the hospitals had maternity wards, but this hospital specialized in maternity care. Today that has changed. Now this same hospital is known as Pittsburgh's largest abortion mill.

Each year in America one and a half million unborn babies are legally slaughtered. This reflects a major crisis in family values. The chief justification for this modern slaughter of innocents is that they are "unwanted children." For a child to be unwanted, his parents assign to him low value. Indeed they consider the child to be a liability rather than an asset.

Sociologists have explained the radical shift in the value of children from ancient cultures to our own day by virtue of the shift from an agricultural economy to an industrial or technological economy. In antiquity a large family, particularly many sons, meant cheap labor in the fields. Now an additional child means an additional economic burden. Parents must pay the cost of food and clothes, and they may also pay for braces and college tuition. We have been told that we simply cannot "afford" to have more than two children.

This economic calculus of the value of children is an exercise in insanity. Imagine speaking in such terms while living in the wealthiest nation in history. Imagine this value judgment in a land where poor people enjoy more amenities and luxuries than most kings who ever lived. What would Henry VIII have given for an electric light or a flush toilet?

Beyond this economic madness is the consideration of the joy and meaning we gain from our children over against our disposable goods. Most of us do not consider our children disposable goods. Most of us would not hesitate to divest ourselves of our cars or stereos in order to save the life of one of our children. Cars and the like may give us some measure of comfort and pleasure, but can they ever take the place of the joy we receive from the hugs of our kids?

I like people. I've met thousands of them in my lifetime. I enjoy my friends. But there is nothing like family. The closest people to me in the world are my family. My greatest griefs have been the loss of family members to death. My greatest joys have been found in relationships with my family.

The arrival of Robert Campbell changes my life. I believe it is a change for the good. The bundle in which he was wrapped when he came home from the hospital is indeed a bundle of joy. It came not from the stork but from the Creator of storks. Campbell already occupies a place of inestimable value in my life.

CHAPTER 10

—⊱⊰—

RAISING
BIBLICALLY
RESPONSIVE
ADULTS

—⊱⊰—

GARY EZZO

The biblical proclamation that sin is passed from parent to child (Prov. 28:7; 2 Chron. 22:3; Josh. 22:24–25) serves to exhort us and to stir up passions about the present and future spiritual welfare of our children. Yet even under the piercing light of the truth, many parents stand back and wait on grace to bring about change. But how can they expect the communications of grace unless they wait on God in the manner prescribed in Scripture? God's promises are rich, insuring against discouragement. Faith in God's promises, however, will not nullify one's parental duty, but stir the soul to perform this duty faithfully.

In my field of endeavor, going from church to church and from house to house, I visit families and observe children and grandchildren. This helps me understand with greater empathy Abraham's words to Abimelech: "Surely, the fear of God is not in this place" (Gen. 20:11). I go to homes where the words of Joshua are enshrined in great plaques: "For me and my house, we will serve the LORD" (Josh. 24:15). But I observe the children and come away asking, "Who is this lord they serve?"

The church today is in desperate need of men, women, parents, and pastors who will rise up and shout to God's slumbering sheep the truths that thundered from Samuel Worcester's New England pulpit in the early 1800s: "If we would obtain for our children the spiritual blessings comprised in the gracious promises of the covenant, we must believe and be faithfully obedient . . . for it is only in the way of obedience that we are to expect the favor of God and the communications of His grace" (Oct. 1811).

Each duty is fashioned by a future goal—eternal, moral, and personal. I want you to know (1) the importance of securing your child's salvation, (2) the way to train him in the ethics of Christ, and (3) the relational goal of parenting.

The ministry of reconciliation is the first duty of parents (2 Cor. 5:18–20), because it is the supreme need of all who have life. What will motivate them to faithfully discharge their duties? They have an appointment with God to give an account for the resource of life with which God entrusted them. When my children were young, I longed for them to know Jesus Christ (John 17:3). How wretched is this age, for we are lulled into thinking that the good day of salvation is to-morrow. Yet the Bible says this: "Fool! This night your soul will be required of you" (Luke 12:20); and "Behold, now is the day of salvation" (2 Cor. 6:2). We must be concerned that our children will set their hope on God and that God's renewing grace will give life to their dead souls. When the earth is no more, the heavens are rolled away, and the uni-verse is dissolved, where will your children be?

The moral goal of parenting is to train them in the ethics of Christ. Today the parents are often more occupied with the child's psychological health than his moral health, more with his happiness than his holiness. As a result and to our shame, the modern church has failed to raise children who are thor-oughly moral (Matt. 23:27). Many children know how to act out the Christian life, but do not live it in its reality. This hap-pens because parents tend to tell their children *what* to do, but fall weak-kneed for the lack of knowledge when it comes to telling them *why* they should do it. Knowing *how* to do right and knowing *why* to do right are distinctly different things. The first speaks to moral action in the present; the second, to a deposit of moral principle for the future.

To complicate the matter, many Christian parents com-municate moral precepts only in moments of conflict. That is, they train primarily in times of correction when suppressing evil and wayward behavior. Suppressing such behavior is im-portant, but when it is done to the exclusion of elevating good, you distort the real meaning of good. When teaching godly principles, these parents tell their children what is wrong and what not to do, rather than what is right and what to do. The path to righteous deeds is left undefined, so the child becomes morally vulnerable, open to the fiery darts of the evil one.

Moral training in the Christian home should equal training in biblical virtues and values. Why should parents teach
their children Christian values? First and foremost, because
these values reflect the person of Christ (John 13:34–35).
Such values arouse within the child a consciousness of God
and eternity.

Second, because biblical values are other-oriented. A child
trained in them is bathed in sensitivity to others—a prereq-
uisite for healthy and enduring relationships. Jesus was other-
oriented and set the standard for the "one anothers" of Scripture. Biblical values produce the moral mandate of Scripture
to love God and your neighbor (Mark 12:28–31).

And third, because God's values, when allowed to dwell
in you, force the world to take notice. A desperate society will
still be watching the Christian message long after it stops listening to it. In a society in which natural family relationships
are being destroyed, we have the greatest opportunity to
model hope through good behavior (Matt. 5:16b). When we
keep our behavior pure, let our light shine in our marriages,
children, and families, and let the excellencies of Christ be
seen in our members, our conduct will not go unnoticed. The
combined testimony of the reality of both our faith and the
gospel will stand in dramatic contrast to the consequences of
sin in the lives of our countrymen (1 Peter 2:12).

Now we come to the third goal of parenting: to enjoy our
children's earthly friendship. To secure a child's friendship, I
suggest a course that is contrary to the wisdom of our day,
but one set in motion by Jesus himself: "No longer do I call
you servants [disciples], for a servant does not know what his
master is doing; but I have called you friends, for all things
that I heard from My Father I have made known to you"

(John 15:15). From the early years of gathering his men right up to the Last Supper, our Lord continually passed on his wisdom to his disciples. As their shepherd, he brought conformity into their thinking by creating a like-mindedness and an identical direction for life. In John 15, the Lord finished discipling his men and entered into a new relationship with them, one he called friendship.

As stewards of God's special gifts, we are called to a discipling relationship with our children—bringing their naïve and foolish ways to maturity and wisdom (Prov. 4:1–7). There will be plenty of time for friendship later, and when parents disciple their children wisely, there will be plenty of reason for it. But friendship with our children is not the starting point of our parenting—it is the relational goal. We begin training our children from the position not of pals or peers, but of parents. Only when we have brought our children to a common like-mindedness (Phil. 2:1–5) of who we are in Christ as a family will we be in a position to enjoy our children and give them a reason to enjoy us.

The duty, hope, and goal of the Christian parent is to raise a morally responsible child who comes to salvation in Jesus Christ, who's life is governed by the precepts of Christ, and who reflects the love of Christ. To obtain for our children the spiritual and saving blessings comprised in the gracious promises of God's Word, we, the governors of their souls, must believe and be faithfully obedient to the revelation. Without faith we have no title to any blessings of promise. Without obedience we cannot expect God to favor or to communicate his grace on either our children or our efforts.

⟨∞⟩

CHAPTER 11

THAT YOU MAY
LIVE LONG

⟨∞⟩

JAMES B. JORDAN

The Holy Spirit tells children to obey their parents in the Lord (Eph. 6:1). This passage quotes Exodus 20:12 and Deuteronomy 5:16: "Honor your father and mother (which is the first commandment with [a] promise), that it may be well with you and [that] you may live long on the earth" (Eph. 6:2–3).

Commentators have debated the sense in which this commandment, the fifth, is "the first commandment with a promise." In fact the second commandment has a promise as well: "Showing mercy to thousands, to those who love Me and keep My commandments" (Exod. 20:6). So the fifth commandment is not really the first one with a promise attached to it. Some have suggested that a better translation would be something like this: "which is a commandment of first-rate importance as concerns promise."

In this short chapter we must set aside this debate and note that those who obey this law receive a blessing. Some people believe that the law's blessings and curses do not apply to believers in the new covenant, but the Spirit clearly contradicts this notion in Ephesians 6:1–3. Here a long and prosperous life is promised as the usual reward of those who honor their earthly parents.

True believers have been freed from the condemnation of the law and have learned to love the law. The law reveals to us God's character. Psalm 119 celebrates our love for God's law. Moreover, the believer seeks new ways to obey and apply God's law, knowing that all Scripture is profitable for instruction in righteousness and equips us for every kind of good work (2 Tim. 3:16–17).

So let us consider first of all what "honor" means. Biblically speaking, honoring is the opposite of repudiating. God himself states in Exodus, "He who curses [literally, repudiates] his father or his mother shall surely be put to death" (Exod. 21:17). Here we see how strongly God feels about this matter. He makes wonderful promises to those who honor their parents, but those who repudiate and reject them he threatens with severe judgment.

Part of honoring parents, as long as the child is under age, is obeying them. A child is to obey his parents unless they command him to break an explicit law of the Lord ("Obey your parents *in the Lord*"). You can read about a rebellious teenager, who was a drunkard and who repudiated his parents, in Deuteronomy 21:18–21. God commanded that such a youth be put to death. God takes honoring parents very seriously.

Though a grown child no longer obeys his parents, he must still honor them (see chap. 12). In 1 Timothy we see that honoring someone means taking care of their financial needs (1 Tim. 5:3–4, 17). Just as the parents cared for the child when he was young, so the grown child must care for his parents in their old age. Jesus said that Pharisees who were failing to care for their parents deserved to be put to death (Mark 7:9–13). As far as he was concerned, refusing to care for one's aged parents is a capital offense.

In these examples we see that younger children are to obey their parents, and that gross, pronounced, repeated disobedience to parents and repudiation of their authority is worthy of death. Second, we see that grown children are to care for their parents and that failure to do so is also a crime worthy of death. Today these sins should be, at the very least, matters of serious church discipline.

Why is this matter so important? Because God designed the human race as his image. To an infant, the faces of his father and mother are God's face. Usually in the late teenage years a Christian child comes to have a personal relationship with Jesus Christ. Before then, the child's relationship with God is mediated through his parents and church. This is how God designed it. As we grow apart from our parents, moving toward the age of 20, we must enter into a new, more direct relationship with God.

When a child disobeys his parents, he disobeys, for all intents and purposes, God himself. When a teenager repudiates his parents, he repudiates God. For obvious reasons this is tremendously serious, and it brings a horrible curse.

By the same token, a child who resists his natural, rebellious tendencies and submits to his parents, is submitting to God, and this brings wonderful blessings.

The story of Absalom, David's son, is the story of a rebellious son (2 Sam. 13–18). David was hardly a perfect father. He had failed to discipline his sons, so they grew up with little restraint (1 Kings 1:6). Absalom's half-brother Amnon, following David's example with Bathsheba, raped Absalom's sister Tamar (2 Sam. 11 and 13), and David did nothing about it. Taking matters into his own hands, Absalom killed Amnon, following David's example with Uriah the Hittite. Then David exiled Absalom and refused to deal with the situation until forced to do so. From all this we see that David was an ineffectual and weak father. Absalom certainly had reasons to be angry.

Yet Absalom should have submitted to David anyway. David had submitted to Saul, even when Saul exiled him and then tried to kill him; David even mourned Saul's death. Absalom, however, was a rebellious son. He conspired against David, overthrew him, and drove him out. But God killed Absalom, just as God had threatened to do to any rebellious son.

We are all Absaloms. God himself was Adam's father. God was both Adam's heavenly Father and his earthly father. He was Adam's parent. Adam repudiated God's parental authority, and God drove him from the Garden. Adam did not live long on the land God had given him. And all of us are like Adam.

There was one Son, however, who obeyed his Father perfectly: the last Adam, Jesus. Not only did Jesus obey his Father, but on the cross Jesus made provisions for his mother, telling John to care for her (John 19:26–27).

One of Jesus' seven last words was devoted to honoring parents!

In union with Christ and by the power of the Holy Spirit, we honor our Father, God, and our Mother, the church. But we must also, if we wish to live and prosper on this earth, honor our earthly parents and guardians.

CHAPTER 12

———∞———

A 30-YEAR-OLD
CHILD

———∞———

R. C. SPROUL, JR.

M y father is most frequently asked this question,
"Where did evil come from?" The question I receive more often than any other is this: "What's it
like to have R. C. Sproul as your father?" I'm not sure which
is harder to answer.

The most weird thing about having R. C. Sproul as your
father is that you're always asked what it's like. It's not as if I
have anything with which to compare it. I don't know if
they're asking about having a father who is well known or
one who is so intelligent. I do know, however, that the burden of being his son has nothing to do with how "famous" he
is, or with how smart he is. These have never been issues.

What has been hard about being his son is the standards

he has set. Don't get me wrong. He is by no means a pushy man. If anything, he took it too easy on my while I was growing up. Rather he set standards by example. I don't worry if I'll ever be as smart as he, I worry if I'll ever be as good. I've never been worried if I'll be a great theologian or a great writer. What worries me is if I'll be a righteous man.

That's the hold my father has on me. He has raised me, educated me, disciplined me. Most importantly, however, he has modeled for me what it means to be a godly man. Our relationship, like all those between father and son, changed dramatically when I became a man. (Before I became a man, he was fond of asking me, "When do you become a man?" I was to respond dutifully, "When you tell me I am a man.") Now he can't spank or ground me; he can't even fire me.

The Bible is rather clear on the responsibility of young children to their parents. The Decalogue promised Jews the blessing of long life in the land if children honored their parents. God's law provided for capital punishment for those children who were recalcitrant in their refusal to obey. The Bible also clearly teaches that a man is to leave his parents and cleave to his wife. When a man marries, he becomes the head of a household. But the Bible is not so clear on how a child should relate to his or her parents after the leaving and cleaving.

Our language suffers from the same ambiguity. Ask any parent how many children he or she has, and they won't stop to separate those at home and those away. I am no longer a child, I am a man. And yet I am one of my parents' children. So which is it?

The culture puts a heavy emphasis on being a man. Individualism has so pervaded our thinking that when a child leaves the nest he is on his own. (The culture, in fact, is loathe to recognize the authority of a father over a child still in the nest.) No longer does a son set up house in the shadow of his father's home. The relationship hangs in limbo for decades until the roles reverse and the son gallantly becomes the father to his enfeebled old dad.

The culture, not surprisingly, is wrong. God has not created us atomistically. He has called us to live, not individually, but in community, as family. As Christians swimming against the cultural stream, trying to shine light into darkness, we must be quick to affirm and recognize the parent's continuing hold over the child. Our current problem is certainly not overbearing parents who refuse to recognize a change in their authority after the leaving and cleaving. Our problem is parents who refuse to counsel and advise, not meddlesome curmudgeons who demand their own way. Our problem is not tyranny, but abdication.

We need young men who are not so zealous for the mantle of authority as to bristle under insights of those experienced sages. We need young men who see their authority not as an excuse for autonomy, but as a test of fidelity. We need young men who are not ashamed to ask for help, who honor their parents even while recognizing that they need not obey them. We need patriarchs, men who will at once recognize the sovereignty of households, yet be quick with wise counsel to those of us still learning. We need to remember that young children are to honor and obey their parents, and that grown children must honor them.

My father doesn't often remember it, but he has an iron grip on me. His control is first in those internalized habits that he ingrained in me as a child. I am like him, I speak like him, I think like him. But his grip is strongest in this: of all my earthly fears none looms larger than the dread that I somehow might disappoint him. And nothing on this earth motivates me more than my desire to make him proud. This is part of what it means to honor.

What's it like to have R. C. Sproul as your father? It's easy, for how many sons have a partriarch to look to with so much wisdom? How many sons can pick up the phone and get an astute answer to a vexing philosophical or exegetical or theological or historical or sports-trivia question? How many sons know that their father is rooting for them, praying for them?

And having a father like R. C. Sproul is also impossible. How many sons are in my shoes, loving their father so much that, no matter how proud he is, no matter how quick he is to tell me, it will never be enough—not for him, but for me?

Adult children, honor your mother and father all the days of your life. Honor them by establishing your home and your authority. But then honor them by inviting them in, seeking out their insights. Honor them by refusing to hoard your authority, and yield to their wisdom and experience. Parents of adult children, play the man. Fill the shoes. Show the world again what it means to be a patriarch and matriarch.

Give them counsel while respecting their authority. Don't let the culture crowd you out. Keep teaching your children well. And know they love you.

APPENDIX 1

—⊗⊗⊗—

PASTORING
MASCULINITY

—⊗⊗⊗—

DOUGLAS WILSON

A number of years ago, a visitor to our church commented on something that struck him as uncommon, or at least more rare than it should be. "The men *pray* ..." he said. Too often the picture of men at church is that of the hapless drone, maneuvered through the doors by a pious wife. He is not exactly spiritual, but he is docile, and that is reckoned to be close enough.

In recent years the church has consequently placed a great deal of emphasis on recovering the concept of biblical masculinity. Much of the discussion has been good and helpful, but an important element has been lacking. We *do* need to talk about the ministry to individual men and encourage them to serve God as men. We may be thankful that such teaching has sought to equip men to function as individual members of their families. At the same time we must be careful that this focus does not backfire, and that we not find ourselves ministering to men as just another subgroup with their own special needs. We have a youth group, we have college and career, and over in the corner we have . . . the men.

We have not yet begun to teach and encourage men to be representatives of their families—or to use the biblical phrase, heads of households. For example, the biblical pattern of evangelism is not at all that of picking up the devil's stragglers, but that of bringing the good news to household after household. Crispus provides just one of many examples: "Then Crispus, the ruler of the synagogue, believed on the Lord with all his household" (Acts 18:8). Not surprisingly, the head of the household played a key role in his household's coming to faith. Why should this change *after* his household comes into the church?

This issue has a direct bearing on the health of every church. Conscious of the fact that large modern churches are too often "impersonal," we often try to restore the personal element through such programs as undershepherds or cell groups. But God has already established a primary system of "undershepherds." They are called fathers and husbands. Ministry that treats fathers and husbands as "just another group" in the church is doomed to fail at shepherding a disconnected crowd of individuals, loners, egalitarians, and democrats. Such is the American church.

Pastors must therefore find a way to encourage and equip men, as the heads of their respective households, to function in a pastoral way in their homes. The duties of a Christian father are clear in Scripture, and they are *pastoral* in nature.

This does not mean setting up a pulpit in the living room, or administering the sacraments around the dinner table. But a father *is* to bring up his children in the nurture and admonition of the Lord. A husband *is* to nourish and cherish his wife, loving her as Christ loved the church. These duties cannot be performed by anyone else in the church, and their performance (or lack of performance) directly affects the health of the church. Sound households are the key to a sound church.

Of course if a man is not being encouraged by his pastor to take this role seriously, the man is not therefore exempt from his duties. A man is responsible to provide this pastoral oversight in his home whether or not others around him are being helpful. At the same time, if a congregation's elders take their task seriously, they can be a tremendous help to those men who want to lead and govern their families responsibly. In turn, this provides a great blessing to the church because it is constituted in line with the Word.

In various ways a pastor can encourage this mindset. First, he can teach the congregation, clearly and forcefully, what the Bible says about the subject. Some commotion may result, but cowardice in the pulpit has never been anointed by God. Second, the elders of a church can discipline themselves to think differently by changing a few expressions. We need to count by fours.

"How many go to your church?"

"We are very grateful—the Lord has given us about 100 households."

And when the men of a church gather (at a meeting or conference), they should be seen, recognized, and addressed as *representing* the church. Because individualism pervades the modern church, we react to such suggestions as an attempt to exclude women and children, rather than as a biblical attempt to include households.

Pastors need to ask themselves a hard question: What role, if any, do households as households perform in the life of our church? Until the question can be answered clearly, the men of the church will not assume the role to which God has called them. Meanwhile, they can still play softball at church picnics.

APPENDIX 2

———— ⚬⚬⚬ ————

THE CHURCH
AND WIDOWS

———— ⚬⚬⚬ ————

DON KISTLER

I f any believing man or woman has widows," writes Paul, "let them relieve them, and do not let the church be burdened, that it may relieve those who are really widows" (1 Tim. 5:16).

Scripture says that the Lord defends widows, that we should plead for them, and that God hears the cries of afflicted widows. We are told in the Old Testament that God blesses those who care for widows and curses those who do not. In the New Testament James makes attending to the needs of widows (and the fatherless) one mark of "pure and undefiled religion" (1:27).

In his commentary on the catechism, the Puritan Thomas Vincent groups together all who lack families and says we should provide for them. James appears to do the same, even adding to the exhortation of financial provision that of visiting—or becoming the spiritual family. This includes emotional and practical support, everything from compassion to car repairs. Clearly God is most compassionate to those on whom his afflicting providence is also greatest.

Following Vincent's lead, we see that the term *widow* here means primarily women whose husbands have died and secondarily any woman left alone without support. It may also include not-yet-adult children (or young adults) who, for a variety of reasons, lack the benefit of parental oversight. In this short space it is impossible to develop fully the exegesis required to demonstrate this, but biblically a widow can be a daughter, a mother, a sister, an aunt, a niece, or anyone who loses a husband through divorce, death, desertion, imprisonment, or any other means.

God is most tender toward widows, those whom Paul calls "really widows" or "widows indeed" (1 Tim. 5:16). The Greek word for *widow* means "bereft, being left alone, and thereby suffering loss." A "widow indeed" identifies a woman who has no relative left to help her.

"Widows indeed" are distinguished from widows with other means of financial support. If the deceased husband has left his wife with the means of support, the church, while it must continue to provide for her spiritual needs, has no financial obligation to her.

Our society assumes that the job of giving "widows indeed" financial support belongs to the state. But 1 Timothy 5:4 teaches that if a widow has descendants or grandchildren, they are responsible to provide for her needs. This is an issue, not of providing to a point of discomfort or inconvenience, but of changing lifestyles. If a widow falls into this category, the obligation is clear: a family must take the responsibility to the extent they are able.

If the need exceeds a family's means, that remaining responsibility rests on the church. One large church in southern California maintains a used-clothing store, the proceeds from which support the widows in that church: single mothers, so they can be keepers at home, as Scripture commands; divorced mothers, for the same reason; and widows indeed, who are in financial straits.

When considering everything on which churches spend their money, one must conclude that few churches accept their obligation to widows. Churches spend thousands of dollars on advertising and technology, while their widows live in poverty.

In *The Widow Directed to the Widows' God*, John Angell James articulates the compassion of Christ for these dear ones: "One of the errands on which the Son of God came from heaven to earth was to bind up the broken-hearted and to comfort all that mourn. How incumbent is it [upon us] to manifest the same tenderness of spirit towards this deeply suffering portion of the human family? A group of children gathered around a widowed mother, and sobbing out their sorrows as she repeats to them amidst many tears their father's loved and honored name, is one of those pictures of woe which few can look [at] with unmoistened eye. Permit me to whisper in your ear and direct your troubled spirit to this passage: 'Let thy widow trust in Me,' Jeremiah 49:11, 'for a judge of the fatherless and the widow is God in His holy habitation,' Psalm 68:5."

APPENDIX 3

---∞---

CHILDREN,
OBEY

---∞---

J. STEVEN WILKINS

When are we going to learn? When will we learn that God's creatures can live successfully in his world only by following his ways? If God is all-wise and all-holy, his Word must be both good (because it is the fruit of unblemished holiness) and best (because it is the fruit of infinite wisdom). If this is so (and it is), why do we persist in seeking other ways?

Life becomes a bewildering labyrinth when we ignore God's truth and seek wisdom from below. Nowhere is this more clearly illustrated than in the family. Why the warfare between parent and child? Why is parenthood so difficult, dreaded, and feared? Why is growing up so painful and distressing? Because we think we are wiser than God.

How clear and simple are his directions to parents and children: "Children, obey your parents in the Lord, for this is right. . . . fathers, do not provoke your children to wrath but bring them up in the training and admonition of the Lord" (Eph. 6:1–4).

Children are to obey. Parents have been given authority by God to command their children. Indeed, parents hold the position of God's representatives to their children. For this reason children are commanded to honor their parents even as they honor the Lord himself (Lev. 19:3; Heb. 12:9). In this antiauthoritarian age we need to remember this. It is not unreasonable to expect obedience from little ones (or our "big, teenage ones" for that matter). The authority they submit to is God's, and his authority ought always to be honored.

The submission required of children is not unlimited, however. No parent has the right to command anything contrary to Scripture. Children are required to obey but only "in the Lord" (Eph. 6:1).

Children are to obey, "for this is right." Paul does not mention the many benefits that come to obedient children, nor does he mention the benefits parents derive from obedient children. He simply points to the ultimate reason we are to do anything—because it is right. It is God's will that you honor your parents. Yes, great blessings come to you (and to them) when you honor them, but the primary reason to do this is that God requires it.

But what about the responsibilities of parents? Mutual privileges and responsibilities mark covenantal relationships. If one party is bound to submit to the authority of another, it is incumbent on the other party to exercise that authority in

lawful, honorable ways. Thus Paul tells fathers, "Do not provoke your children to wrath" (Eph. 6:4).

This does not mean we will never make our children angry. Being sinners, children are selfish and sometimes become
angry even when we exercise authority properly. The point is
that fathers are not to provoke anger by ungodly rule. When
we give unscriptural commands, when we make unjust demands, when our expectations for our children are unreasonable, when our chastisements are too harsh or too lax, when
we administer our rule hypocritically or inconsistently, our
rule is ungodly.

If our children are provoked to anger by faithful rule, they
sin. If they are provoked by inconsistent or unreasonable rule,
we have sinned.

We must not provoke our children but rather "bring them
up in the training and admonition of the Lord" (Eph. 6:4). We
must rule over them as God rules over us. Because he nurtures
and admonishes us, we must instruct, encourage, and lead, as
well as chasten, rebuke, and correct, our children. We must set
before them the truth of God and train them to walk in it.

This is not profound. It does not come from a densely
printed, heavily footnoted, professional treatise. You won't
find these things in the latest psychology journals. But these
simple directives are God's formula for a happy home. Following these, children will receive the promised blessings of
the covenant (it will "be well with you and you may live long
on the earth" [Eph. 6:3]). You won't be injured by submitting
to your parents. They are protectors whom God has set over
you for your good.

Obeying this, parents will enjoy the blessing of children
who love and honor them, and even more importantly, who

love and honor the God who made them. "Correct your son, and he will give you rest; yes, he will give delight to your soul" (Prov. 29:17). You don't have to worry about warping your children if you spank them as God commands. You don't have to fear inhibiting their creativity by insisting on obedience to your word. You need not fear wounding their "self-esteem" by saying no. If God commands us to do these things, we know they can be done safely.

Children are blessings, not burdens (Ps. 127:3). Children should prize, not despise, their parents (Prov. 17:6). Why continue domestic warfare? Forget the threats; discard the nasty words; abandon the bribery, manipulation, and deception; dry your tears; and begin, by God's grace, to do what he says. Then and only then will you dwell safely and securely and enjoy covenant peace.